T0413614

Making Difficult Words Easy

Code Reader Books provide codes with "sound keys" to help read difficult words. For example, a word that may be difficult to read is "unicorn," so it might be followed by a code like this: unicorn *(YOO-nih-korn)*. By providing codes with phonetic sound keys, Code Reader Books make reading easier and more enjoyable.

Examples of Code Reader™ Keys

Long a sound (as in make):
a *(with a silent e)* or **ay**
Examples: able *(AY-bul)*; break *(brake)*

Short i sound (as in sit): **i** or **ih**
Examples: myth *(mith)*; mission *(MIH-shun)*

Long i sound (as in by):
i *(with a silent e)* or **y**
Examples: might *(mite)*; bicycle *(BY-sih-kul)*

Keys for the long o sound (as in hope):
o *(with a silent e)* or **oh**
Examples: molten *(MOLE-ten)*; ocean *(OH-shen)*

Codes use dashes between syllables *(SIH-luh-buls)*, and stressed syllables have capital letters.

To see more Code Reader sound keys, see page 44.

BIGFOOT AND THE LOCH (lock) NESS MONSTER

TREASURE BAY

Bigfoot and the Loch Ness Monster

A Code Reader™ Chapter Book

Blue Series

This book, along with images and text, is published under license from The Creative Company. Originally published by as Bigfoot and Loch Ness Monster

Additions and revisions to text in this licensed edition:

Additional images provided by iStock

Reading Consultant: Jennifer L. VanSlander, Ph.D., Asst. Professor of Educational Leadership, Columbus State University

Published by
Treasure Bay, Inc.
PO Box 519
Roseville, CA 95661 USA

Printed in China

Library of Congress Control Number: 2024944835

ISBN: 978-1-60115-720-1

Visit us online at:
CodeReader.org

PR-1-25

CONTENTS

1 CRYPTOZOOLOGY *(krip-toh-zoo-AH-luh-jee)*

What is cryptozoology *(krip-toh-zoo-AH-luh-jee)*, and where did it come from?

Sometime in the 1950s, a scholar *(SKAH-lur)* named Bernard Heuvelmans *(HEE-vul-munz)* was studying animals when he began to realize that known animals were not interesting enough for him. So he began researching *(REE-sur-ching)* animals of legend instead. These are animals that some people say they have seen, but that have never been captured *(KAP-churd)* or proven to be real.

Heuvelmans's *(HEE-vul-munz)* goal was to evaluate *(ee-VAL-yoo-ate)* the possibility that these animals actually *(AK-choo-uh-lee)* existed. He called this new field of study "cryptozoology *(krip-toh-zoo-AH-luh-jee)*" and called the animals "cryptids *(KRIP-tids)*."

There are many cryptids around the world, such as the chupacabra *(choo-puh-KAH-brah)* in South America, the Yeti *(YET-ee)* in Asia *(AY-zhuh)*, and werewolves *(WAIR-wulvz)* in Europe *(YUR-rup)*. But perhaps the two most famous *(FAY-mus)* of these animal legends are the ape-like forest creature *(KREE-chur)* Bigfoot and the giant, lake-dwelling creature, the Loch *(lock)* Ness Monster.

2 LET'S START WITH BIGFOOT

For centuries *(SEN-chur-eez)*, people have told stories of Bigfoot living deep in the forests of North America. Bigfoot is said to be a huge, hairy figure *(FIG-yur)* that walks like a human *(HYOO-mun)* and leaves huge footprints.

But what is it? An ape? A species *(SPEE-sheez)* of human that somehow escaped scientific *(sy-en-TIF-ik)* notice? A man, too embarrassed *(em-BARE-ust)* by his immense size, hairy body, and big feet to allow himself to be seen? These are questions that cryptozoologists *(krip-toh-zoo-AH-luh-jists)* hope to answer *(AN-sur)*.

According to those who claim to have seen one, a Bigfoot could be seven to eight feet tall. They may be covered with black, brown, or reddish hair on all but their face, palms, and feet. Some say a Bigfoot can scream, grunt, or moan but most often makes a whistling *(WIS-ling)* sound.

A Bigfoot's smell is distinctively *(dis-TINKT-tiv-lee)* awful—like rotten eggs. Maybe that's why, in Florida, this type of cryptid *(KRIP-tid)* is also called a Skunk Ape!

This type of creature is thought to be very fast, having been clocked running alongside vehicles *(VEE-hik-ulz)* at 45 to 70 miles per hour. Their eyes seem to glow red, pink, green, or white in the dark, with what appears to be their own light. Their hands are believed *(bee-LEEVD)* to be like those of orangutans *(uh-RANG-uh-tanz)* and humans, with four long fingers and an opposable *(uh-POZE-uh-bul)* thumb.

Bigfoot (the plural of Bigfoot is "Bigfoot," just as more than one moose is called "moose") apparently *(uh-PARE-runt-lee)* eat just about anything: roots, berries *(BARE-eez)*, nuts, pine needles, and even rodents *(ROH-dents)*, rabbits, or chickens.

But where do Bigfoot sleep? Can they climb *(klime)* trees? How long do they live? Can one Bigfoot communicate *(kuh-MYOO-nih-kate)* with another? If they resemble *(ree-ZEM-buhl)* humans so much, why don't they seek out contact with us?

A Bigfoot is said to have exceptionally *(ex-SEP-shun-uh-lee)* large feet and has supposedly *(sup-POZE-ed-lee)* left thousands of oversized footprints throughout forests in the United States and Canada *(KAN-uh-duh)*.

The first known footprints were found in 1958 by workers building *(BIL-ding)* a road deep in the dense forests of northern California *(kal-ih-FORN-yuh)*. One of the workers made plaster casts of the prints. Pictures of the 16-inch-long footprints showed up on the front page of the local newspaper, and the name Bigfoot was born.

Footprints found in forest floors are often several inches deep. That means that the creature that made them could have weighed *(wade)* from several hundred up to 1,000 pounds. Plaster casts made from some of these footprints can be found in colleges *(KOL-uh-jez)*, universities *(yoo-nih-VER-sih-teez)*, research offices, and the basements of Bigfoot chasers.

BIGFOOT SIGHTINGS 3

Roger *(RAH-jur)* Patterson was a former rodeo *(ROH-dee-oh)* rider with a deep interest in Bigfoot. In 1967, he and a friend took a movie camera *(KAM-ur-uh)* and set out to find proof of this forest-dwelling cryptid's existence. They rode on horseback into an area *(AIR-ree-uh)* where there had been many sightings over the years.

There they used their camera to shoot what is now a very famous short film that they claim shows the legendary *(LEJ-un-dare-ee)* creature. It is the only clear photographic *(foh-toh-GRAF-ik)* image *(IM-ij)* of a Bigfoot ever recorded.

There have been hundreds of Bigfoot sightings reported. One story tells of two fur trappers in the late 1800s who claim they were followed through the woods by a smelly, two-legged creature. Each day, when they returned from checking their traps, they found their camp destroyed. One night, one of the trappers heard a commotion *(kuh-MOH-shun)* outside his tent. He fired his shotgun, and whatever it was ran off. The next day, this same trapper returned from checking traps to find his partner dead with a broken neck.

Another story involved five miners *(MY-nurz)* in a cabin on Washington's Mount Saint Helens in 1924. One day, one of the miners saw a Bigfoot and fired at it. That night, their cabin was attacked by several Bigfoot, one of which even punched through the wall. The attack lasted five hours. Although that story was later dismissed as simply not true, it caused *(cawzd)* enough excitement at the time that the area was named Ape Canyon *(KAN-yun)*.

Still another story tells of a logger who was vacationing *(vay-KAY-shun-ning)* in British Columbia *(koh-LUM-bee-uh)*. One night, he was taken from his campsite and dragged for three hours in his sleeping bag. At dawn, he found himself in a camp with a family of Bigfoot. Here he was closely watched for six days until he offered the 8-foot-tall adult male Bigfoot his tin of tobacco *(tuh-BAK-oh)*. The Bigfoot ate it and, either *(EE-thur)* sick or disgusted, ran off to a creek for a drink. That's when the logger escaped.

4 OTHER BIG APE-MEN

Bigfoot is just one of many "ape-men" to have been sighted in remote areas around the world. Its most famous cousin *(KUH-zin)* is probably the yeti *(YET-tee)*, thought to roam the rugged, tall peaks of the Himalaya *(him-uh-LAY-uh)* Mountains of Tibet, Nepal *(nuh-PAHL),* China *(CHY-nuh)*, India *(IN-dee-uh)*, and Pakistan. The yeti is also known as the Abominable *(uh-BAH-min-nuh-bul)* Snowman, although the Tibetan word *yeti* more accurately *(AK-yur-ut-lee)* means "wild man of the snows."

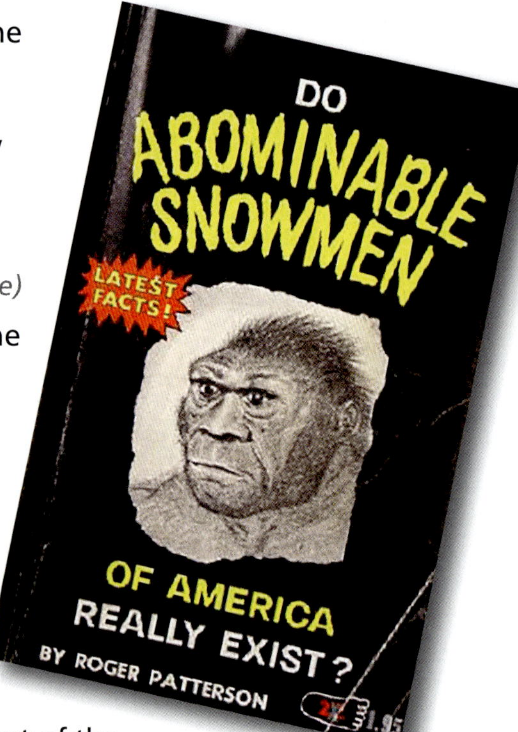

The yeti is said to be a shaggy, stooped creature that lives in caves high in the Himalaya *(him-uh-LAY-uh)* Mountains. But, as with Bigfoot, most of the evidence *(EH-vid-dens)* is based on footprints.

Artist's idea of what the Yeti looks like

Some researchers *(REE-sur-churz)* think the footprints found high in the Himalayas *(him-uh-LAY-uhz)* were actually *(AK-choo-uh-lee)* made by monks walking from one valley to another. A few yeti hunters claim to have found fur from this cryptid. But it is more likely to be fur from a native *(NAY-tiv)* goat known as a serow *(SARE-oh)*.

There have also been sightings in Australia *(aw-STRAY-lee-uh)* of a large, reclusive *(reh-KLOO-siv)*, hairy figure. The yowie *(YOW-ee)* is reported to be eight feet tall with long arms and humanlike hands. Like Bigfoot, it's been described as having a repulsive *(ree-PUL-siv)* body odor *(OH-dur)* similar to rotting garbage *(GAR-bij)*. It also has glowing eyes like Bigfoot. But it is said to be less fearful of human contact. In fact, it's often reported peering in windows or following people in the woods.

Modern-day encounters with Bigfoot-like creatures seem more common, perhaps because people are less embarrassed *(em-BARE-ust)* to share their stories. For example:

- In 1969, an Indiana *(in-dee-AN-uh)* farmer watched a tall, hairy creature with human-like hands for about 2 minutes at a distance of about 25 feet, before it ran off.
- Randy and Lou *(loo)* Rogers *(RAH-jurz)* were visited several times by a large hairy "gorilla" at their Indiana home in the summer of 1972. A nearby farmer claimed it ripped apart nearly 200 of his chickens.

- In 1965, a 17-year-old girl from Michigan *(MISH-uh-gun)* said she got a black eye when a 7-foot-tall hairy giant stepped into the road in front of her car, reached in, and grabbed her. She screamed, and the creature ran off.

- In 1975, an Oklahoma *(oke-luh-HOME-uh)* farmer reported seeing a pair of hairy creatures with glowing eyes and smelling like rotten eggs.

- Between 1977 and 1993, people in Tuscola *(tus-KOH-luh)* County, Michigan, reported seeing hairy bipeds *(BY-pedz)* 38 different times. That's more than two sightings per year!

Bigfoot: This Exit

Bigfoot is known as a shadowy creature who lives deep in the woods where it's rarely seen. But it's a familiar *(fuh-MIL-yur)* and big attraction *(uh-TRAK-shun)* in Willow Creek, California, a place nicknamed "The Gateway to Bigfoot Country."

Willow Creek is a town in northwestern California along the Klamath *(KLAM-uth)* River and about 20 miles south of Bluff Creek, where the famous footprints were sighted in 1958. Bigfoot has left a mark on the city bigger than any footprints.

Several carved statues *(STACH-ooz)* keep watch over the comings and goings of townspeople and tourists *(TOOR-rists).* One stands at the turn to the Bigfoot Scenic *(SEE-nik)* Byway, an 89-mile road through the Salmon *(SAM-un)* Mountains that is regarded as prime Bigfoot country.

However, the main attraction in Willow Creek for Bigfoot seekers may be the Bigfoot Museum *(myoo-ZEE-um)*, which is guarded (*GAR-ded)* by another gigantic *(jy-GAN-tik)* statue. The museum has a collection of photos, footprint casts, press clippings, maps, and, of course, souvenir *(soo-vuh-NEER)* T-shirts.

WHAT ABOUT THE LOCH *(lock)* NESS MONSTER?

5

Halfway around the world, in Scotland, lives another legendary cryptid: the Loch *(lock)* Ness Monster. Nessie, as she is often called, is said to live in a loch *(lock)* called Loch Ness. (Loch is the Scottish word for "lake.") This lake is 24 miles long but only 1 mile wide. That might seem small for such a famous body of water, but Loch Ness is extremely *(ex-STREEM-lee)* deep and holds more water than any other lake in Great Britain *(BRIT-un)*.

The Loch Ness monster seems to want to have nothing to do with people. And that only adds to its mystique *(mis-TEEK)*. There have been thousands of sightings, but for the most part, Nessie has eluded *(ee-LOO-ded)* photographers, filmmakers, sonar *(SOH-nar)* trackers, and serious *(SEE-ree-us)* researchers. Though estimated at times to be as large as 40 feet long, it has appeared only as a dark, moving figure on or in the water—here now and gone an instant later.

People who claim to have seen the Loch Ness Monster describe it in different ways. Sometimes it's a small head and long neck sticking out of the water. Sometimes it looks like a horse's head. Sometimes it's just a few humps moving rapidly through the water. Its color is most often dark gray or black, but sometimes it's lighter. It's typically *(TIP-ik-lee)* 20 to 40 feet long.

Indeed, if any creature wanted to hide from people, Loch Ness would be a good place to do it. Sunlight can penetrate only a few feet into the brown water, so the depths are extremely dark.

People looking for Nessie in recent *(REE-sent)* years have found, in various *(VARE-ee-us)* places on the lakebed, circles *(SUR-kulz)* of rocks and stones, which were constructed by people who lived in the area *(AIR-ree-uh)* just after the last ice age. But no evidence of a monster. Not even so much as a bone.

Naturalists *(NACH-ur-uh-lists)* and others have said that, instead of being some kind of water monster, Nessie is far more likely just be driftwood or other floating debris *(deh-BREE)*. Or, they say, it could be a trail of water left by a passing boat, since waves tend to bounce off the steep shores of the narrow lake and create unusual *(un-YOO-zhoo-ul)* patterns and peaks on the water.

Mirages *(muh-RAH-zhez)* have fooled many on Loch Ness, and they occur *(uh-KUR)* under the same conditions *(kun-DISH-unz)* as Nessie sightings commonly do. In fact, quiet *(KWY-et)*, windless weather *(WEH-thur)* is known around northeastern Scotland as "Nessie weather." Cold air can sometimes cause distant objects to appear larger or stretched upward. This can make small swimming creatures look as though they are much bigger.

The animal most often mistaken for the Loch Ness Monster is probably the European *(YUR-ruh-PEE-un)* otter. The otter is a long, sleek, thick-necked, short-legged animal that is at home both on land and in water. They can only grow to 3 feet long, not including *(in-KLOO-ding)* their tails, so they're not huge. But they often travel in family groups *(groops)*, which may cause observers to mistake them for the humps of a monster.

6 NESSIE SIGHTINGS

Some researchers insist that the people who claimed to have seen a monster in Loch Ness can't all be wrong. Members of the International *(in-tur-NASH-uh-nul)* Society *(suh-SY-ih-tee)* for Cryptozoology *(krip-toh-zoo-AH-luh-jee)* believe there is some sort of giant creature in the lake.

Based on what witnesses have said, they've concluded *(kun-KLOO-ded)* that Nessie could be a plesiosaur *(PLEEZ-ee-uh-sor)*, an animal thought to have gone extinct millions of years ago. Plesiosaurs *(PLEEZ-ee-uh-sorz)* were long-necked, round-bodied sea reptiles measuring *(MEH-zhur-ring)* about 60 feet long, with small, horse-like heads.

Sightings of Nessie started as long ago as the sixth century *(SEN-chur-ee)* when an Irish missionary *(MISH-uh-nair-ee)* ordered a "monster" to stop attacking a swimmer in the loch. Many more stories followed. For example:

- In 1715, a military supply road was built along the south side of the lake. Soldiers *(SOLE-jurz)* building the road reported seeing two creatures "big as whales."
- In 1856, some tourists claimed to have seen a 40-foot-long eel-like creature.
- In 1933, there were 20 sightings of Nessie, and there have been thousands more since then.

Artist's drawing of plesiosaurs

The first highly publicized *(PUB-lih-sized)* sighting happened in the spring of 1933. A husband *(HUZ-bind)* and wife were driving along the shore when they spotted a whale-like creature out in the middle of the water. A newspaper article was written about the sighting. It used the term Loch Ness Monster for the first time.

One classic photographic *(foh-toh-GRAF-ik)* image of the Loch Ness Monster shows a huge creature swimming with its head high above the water atop a long neck. The photo appeared in a London newspaper in 1934. It instantly created a global *(GLOH-bul)* sensation *(sen-SAY-shun)*!

But because the photo was blurry, and it was hard to tell the size of what was in the photo, some researchers were suspicious *(sus-PISH-us)*. Sixty years later, it was revealed to be fake.

In 1960, a cryptozoologist *(krip-toh-zoo-AH-luh-jist)* named Tim Dinsdale got the first motion picture images of the monster. He filmed it for 4 minutes as the creature swam away from him and then up the opposite *(AH-pah-sit)* shore at about 10 miles per hour.

Two decades later, the film was closely scrutinized *(SKROO-tih-nized)* by researchers, and in 1987, they announced their findings. The "monster" had simply been a boat obscured *(ub-SKYURD)* by glare.

IS NESSIE ALONE? OTHER BIG WATER MONSTERS

7

Nessie may be the most famous "water monster," but similar cryptids have been sighted in over 300 lakes around the world.

One of the Great Lakes, Lake Erie *(EE-ree)*, is said to contain a monster known as South Bay Bessie. Bessie has been regularly *(REG-yoo-lur-lee)* sighted since the 1790s. In 1998, a family spotted something in the water about 500 feet offshore. Bubbles gave way to a long ripple and then to three black humps, which appeared to be part of a moving, living creature. Or could it have been driftwood, or boat wakes? As with Nessie, each sighting creates *(kree-ATES)* more mysteries *(MIS-tur-reez)*.

Canada's *(KAN-uh-duz)* version of Nessie is known as Ogopogo *(oh-goh-POH-goh)*. According to legend, Ogopogo lives in Lake Okanagan *(OH-kin-AH-gin)*, in British Columbia *(koh-LUM-bee-uh)*. Ogopogo is said to have special *(SPEH-shul)* powers and is even credited with being able *(AY-bul)* to control the weather.

In 2004, a family sleeping aboard a houseboat on the lake was awakened by a thumping on the boat. The owner of the boat grabbed a camera and recorded what looked to be a 15-foot-long slimy *(SLY-mee)*, greenish-black animal with several humps, swimming about 50 feet away.

Lake Champlain *(sham-PLANE)*, in upstate New York, has had many reports of a long, serpent-like creature poking above the lake's surface and even crawling ashore. In 1873, some railroad workers claim to have seen a serpent with an enormous *(ee-NOR-mus)* head approaching them from the lake. Within days, there were rumors *(ROO-murz)* of cattle being killed and dragged into the water.

8 SEEKING THE TRUTH

In today's world, creatures like Bigfoot and Nessie may no longer be able to avoid *(uh-VOYD)* us. With people finding more ways to explore and work in remote areas, places for Bigfoot to hide are disappearing, and Nessie may no longer be able to appear and disappear at will.

Some researchers have recognized *(REK-ug-nized)* that, while the odds are against *(uh-GENST)* Nessie or a family of Bigfoot turning up, science *(SY-ens)* is required *(ree-KWY-urd)* to consider possibilities. It's a farfetched notion *(NOH-shun)* that a massive beast could have survived in a Scottish loch millions of years after its relatives vanished—or that a creature as large as Bigfoot could be hunted by so many for so long and not be found. But as long as they remain a mystery, people are likely to keep pursuing them.

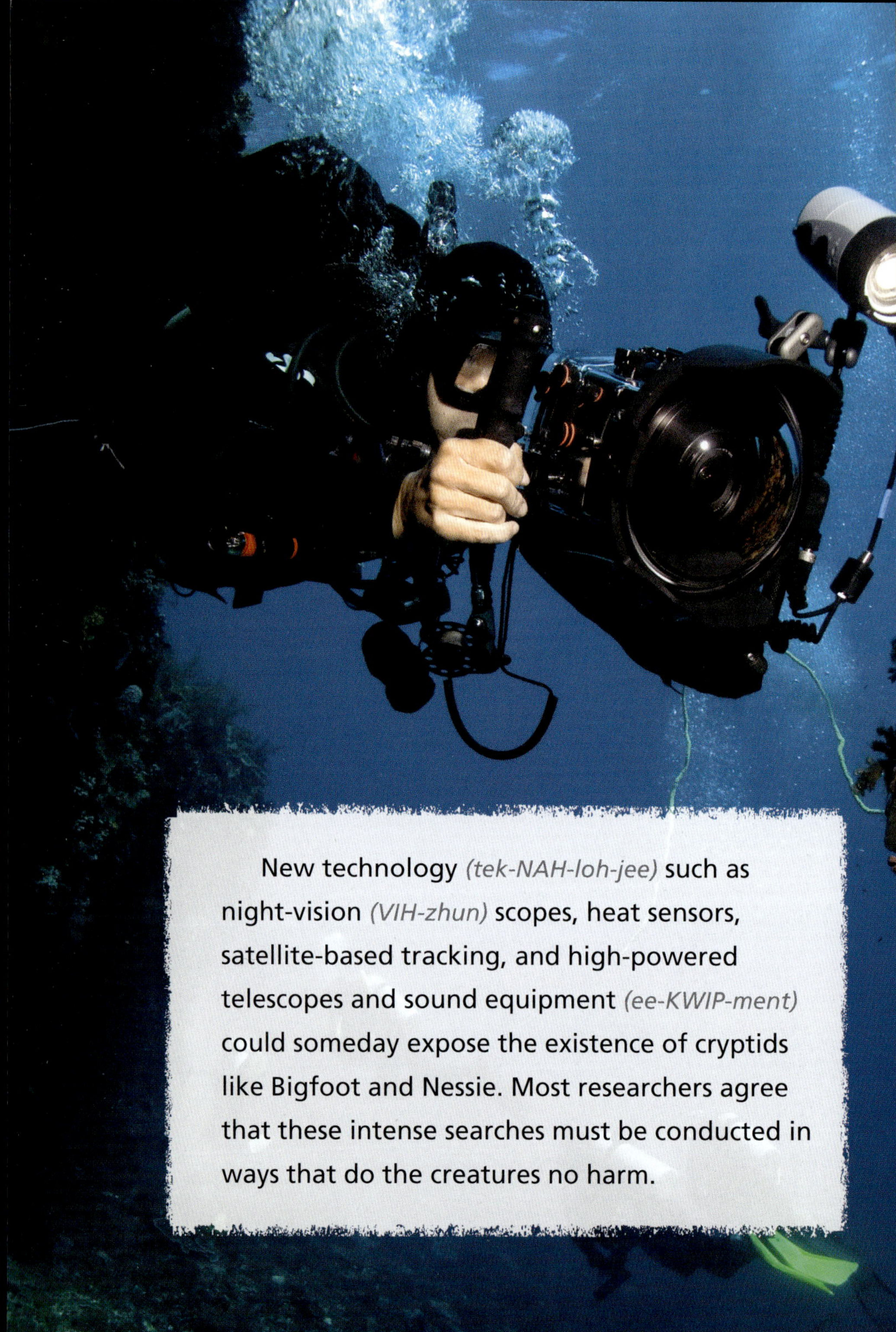

New technology *(tek-NAH-loh-jee)* such as night-vision *(VIH-zhun)* scopes, heat sensors, satellite-based tracking, and high-powered telescopes and sound equipment *(ee-KWIP-ment)* could someday expose the existence of cryptids like Bigfoot and Nessie. Most researchers agree that these intense searches must be conducted in ways that do the creatures no harm.

In 1987, Operation *(op-ur-RAY-shun)* Deepscan used 20 boats in a line, dropping what they called a "curtain *(KUR-ten)* of sonar *(SOH-nar)*" through Loch Ness to try to prove the existence of Nessie. They identified some kind of swimming creature, larger than a shark but smaller than a whale. But they couldn't determine exactly what it was. Years of further exploration *(ex-plor-RAY-shun)* turned up nothing.

Take a Second Look

Binoculars *(bih-NOK-yoo-lurz)*, a video *(VID-ee-oh)* camera, a boat, a sonar unit—all of these things may be important when it comes to sighting these legendary creatures. But so is something called "expectant attention *(uh-TEN-shun)*." Expectant attention is a psychological *(sy-koh-LAH-jih-kul)* condition in which a person sees something unusual only because he has recently become aware that it might be there. The sightings of unidentified aerial *(AIR-ee-ul)* phenomenon (UAP) are frequently *(FREE-kwent-lee)* the result of expectant attention, and many sightings of Nessie or Bigfoot might be as well.

A similar psychological phenomenon *(fuh-NOM-uh-non)* is pareidolia *(pair-ay-DOH-lee-uh),* or thinking that an abstract sound or image is something recognizable. Seeing faces in clouds, human figures in rocks, or animals in blots of ink are examples of pareidolia *(pair-ay-DOH-lee-uh)*, in which the brain fits familiar *(fuh-MIL-yur)* details to something unfamiliar.

When a photo was taken of something below the water in Loch Ness, people thought it might be the face of the Loch Ness Monster. But that could have been pareidolia at work. Later, explorers in the same area found a sunken log with a pattern on the end that looked just like the image in the photo.

Are these cryptids real or not real? No one knows for sure yet. But considering that remains of prehistoric *(pree-his-TORE-ik)* *T. rex* were not discovered until the late 1800s, and many new animal species *(SPEE-sheez)* are discovered around the world every year, some think that proof of Bigfoot, the Loch Ness Monster, and many other cryptids is simply yet to be found. Until then, many cryptozoologists *(krip-toh-zoo-AH-luh-jists)* and many curious *(KYUR-ee-us)* people will continue *(kun-TIN-yoo)* the search for these elusive *(ee-LOO-siv)* animals.

GLOSSARY

casts: reproductions or impressions *(im-PRESH-shunz)* of objects or images, often made with plaster

cryptozoology ***(krip-toh-zoo-AHL-uh-jee)*****:** the study of reports and other evidence of animals unrecognized by most scientists.

evidence ***(EH-vid-dens)*****:** facts or information that proves something is true

legends: traditional stories that are sometimes popularly considered history but are not proven to be factual

loch ***(lock)*****:** another word for lake

mirage ***(mur-RAHZH)*****:** an illusion *(il-LOO-zhun)* caused by light passing through air of different temperatures, such as the appearance of water on a hot surface

pareidolia ***(pair-ay-DOH-lee-uh)*****:** seeing a specific, often meaningful image in a random visual pattern, such as a cloud or an ink spot.

phenomenon ***(fuh-NOM-uh-non)*****:** an occurrence that can be observed

sonar ***(SOH-nar)*****:** a technique *(tek-NEEK)* using sound waves to navigate, find, or communicate with other objects under water, derived from the words "sound navigation and ranging"

QUESTIONS TO THINK ABOUT

1. What are cryptozoologists *(krip-toh-zoo-AH-luh-jists)*, and what are some of the ways they do their research?

2. What kinds of evidence of these creatures have cryptozoologists found?

3. What kind of evidence do you think would need to be found to prove the existence of Bigfoot or the Loch Ness Monster?

4. What, if any, are some other strange cryptids that you have heard of?

5. Have you ever seen or heard something that you could not explain?

Making Difficult Words Easy

Code Reader Books provide codes with "sound keys" to help read difficult words. For example, a word that may be challenging to read is "chameleon," so it might be followed by a code like this: chameleon *(kuh-MEE-lee-un)*.

The codes use phonetic keys for each sound in the word. Knowing the keys can help make reading the codes easier.

Code Reader™ Keys

Long a sound (as in make):
a (with a silent e), **ai**, **ay**
Examples: break *(brake)*;
area *(AIR-ee-uh)*; able *(AY-bul)*

Short a sound (as in cat): **a**
Example: practice *(PRAK-tis)*

Long e sound (as in keep): **ee**
Example: complete *(kum-PLEET)*

Short e sound (as in set): **e** or **eh**
Examples: metric *(MEH-trik)*;
bread *(bred)*

Long i sound (as in by):
i (with a silent e) or **y**
Examples: might *(mite)*;
bicycle *(BY-sih-kul)*

Short i sound (as in sit): **i** or **ih**
Examples: myth *(mith)*;
condition *(kun-DIH-shun)*

Long u sound (as in cube): **yoo**
Example: unicorn *(YOO-nih-korn)*

Short u or schwa sound (as in cup):
u or **uh**
Examples: pension *(PEN-shun)*;
about *(uh-BOWT)*

Long o sound (as in hope):
o (with a silent e), **oh**,
or **o** at the end of a syllable
Examples: molten *(MOLE-ten)*;
ocean *(OH-shen)*; nobody *(NO-bah-dee)*

Short o sound (as in top): **o** or **ah**
Examples: posture *(POS-chur)*;
bother *(BAH-ther)*

Long oo sound (as in cool): **oo**
Example: school *(skool)*

Short oo sound (as in look): **o͝o**
Examples: wood *(wo͝od)*;
could *(ko͝od)*

oy sound (as in boy): **oy**
Example: boisterous *(BOY-stur-us)*

ow sound (as in cow): **ow**
Example: discount *(DIS-kownt)*

aw sound (as in paw): **aw**
Example: faucet *(FAW-sit)*

qu sound (as in quit): **kw**
Example: question *(KWES-chun)*

zh sound (as in garage): **zh**
Example: fission *(FIH-zhun)*